OCT 1 2 2019

WITHDRAWN FROM LIBRARY

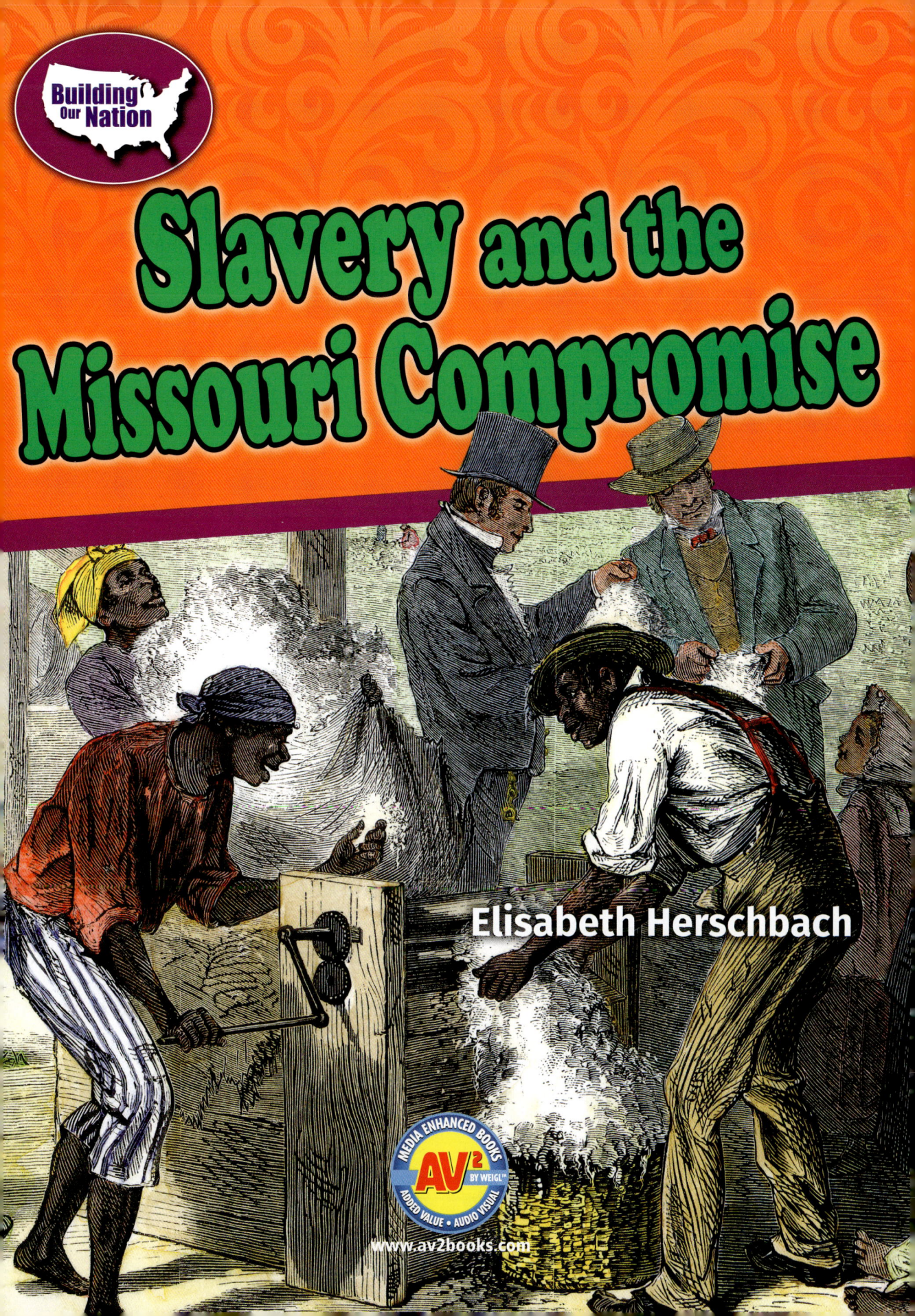

Building Our Nation

Slavery and the Missouri Compromise

Elisabeth Herschbach

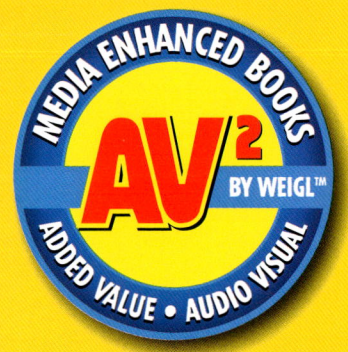

AV² provides enriched content that supplements and complements this book. Weigl's AV² books strive to create inspired learning and engage young minds in a total learning experience.

Your AV² Media Enhanced books come alive with...

 **Audio** Listen to sections of the book read aloud.

 **Key Words** Study vocabulary, and complete a matching word activity.

 **Video** Watch informative video clips.

 **Quizzes** Test your knowledge.

 **Embedded Weblinks** Gain additional information for research.

 **Slide Show** View images and captions, and prepare a presentation.

 **Try This!** Complete activities and hands-on experiments.

Go to www.av2books.com, and enter this book's unique code.

BOOK CODE

AVG93526

AV² by Weigl brings you media enhanced books that support active learning.

... and much, much more!

Published by AV² by Weigl
350 5th Avenue, 59th Floor
New York, NY 10118
Website: www.av2books.com

Copyright © 2020 AV² by Weigl
All rights reserved. No part of this publication may be reproduced, stored in a retrieval system, or transmitted in any form or by any means, electronic, mechanical, photocopying, recording, or otherwise, without the prior written permission of the publisher.

Library of Congress Cataloging-in-Publication Data
Names: Herschbach, Elisabeth, author.
Title: Slavery and the Missouri Compromise / Elisabeth Herschbach.
Description: New York, NY : AV2 by Weigl, [2020] | Series: Building our nation | Audience: K-3.
Identifiers: LCCN 2018053441 (print) | LCCN 2018054380 (ebook) | ISBN 9781489698889 (Multi User ebook) | ISBN 9781489698896 (Single User ebook) | ISBN 9781489698865 (hardcover : alk. paper) | ISBN 9781489698872 (softcover : alk. paper)
Subjects: LCSH: Missouri compromise--Juvenile literature.
Classification: LCC E373 (ebook) | LCC E373 .H47 2020 (print) | DDC 973.5/4--dc23
LC record available at https://lccn.loc.gov/2018053441

Printed in Guangzhou, China
1 2 3 4 5 6 7 8 9 0   23 22 21 20 19

012019
102318

Project Coordinator: John Willis   Designer: Ana María Vidal

Every reasonable effort has been made to trace ownership and to obtain permission to reprint copyright material. The publishers would be pleased to have any errors or omissions brought to their attention so that they may be corrected in subsequent printings.
Weigl acknowledges Alamy, Bridgeman Images, and Getty Images as its primary image suppliers for this title.

First published in 2019 by North Star Editions

CONTENTS

AV² Book Code 2

CHAPTER 1
Slavery in an
Expanding Nation 4

CHAPTER 2
A Heated Debate 10

CHAPTER 3
Drawing a Line 16

CHAPTER 4
A Short-Lived Solution 22

VOICES FROM THE PAST
Frederick Douglass 28

Quiz 30

Key Words/Index 31

Log on to
www.av2books.com 32

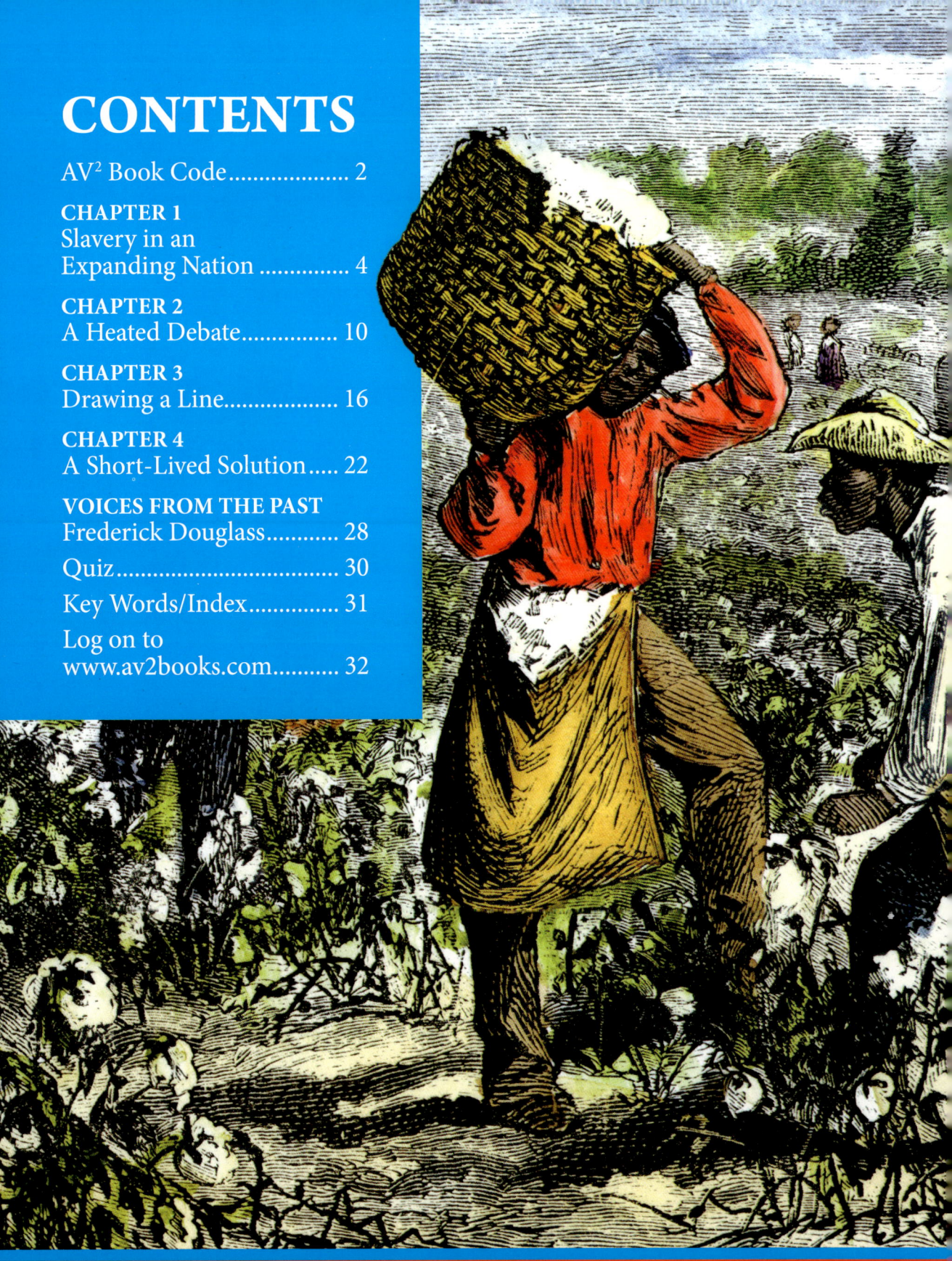

Slavery and the Missouri Compromise

Officials finalized the transfer of the Louisiana Purchase land in December 1803.

4 Building Our Nation

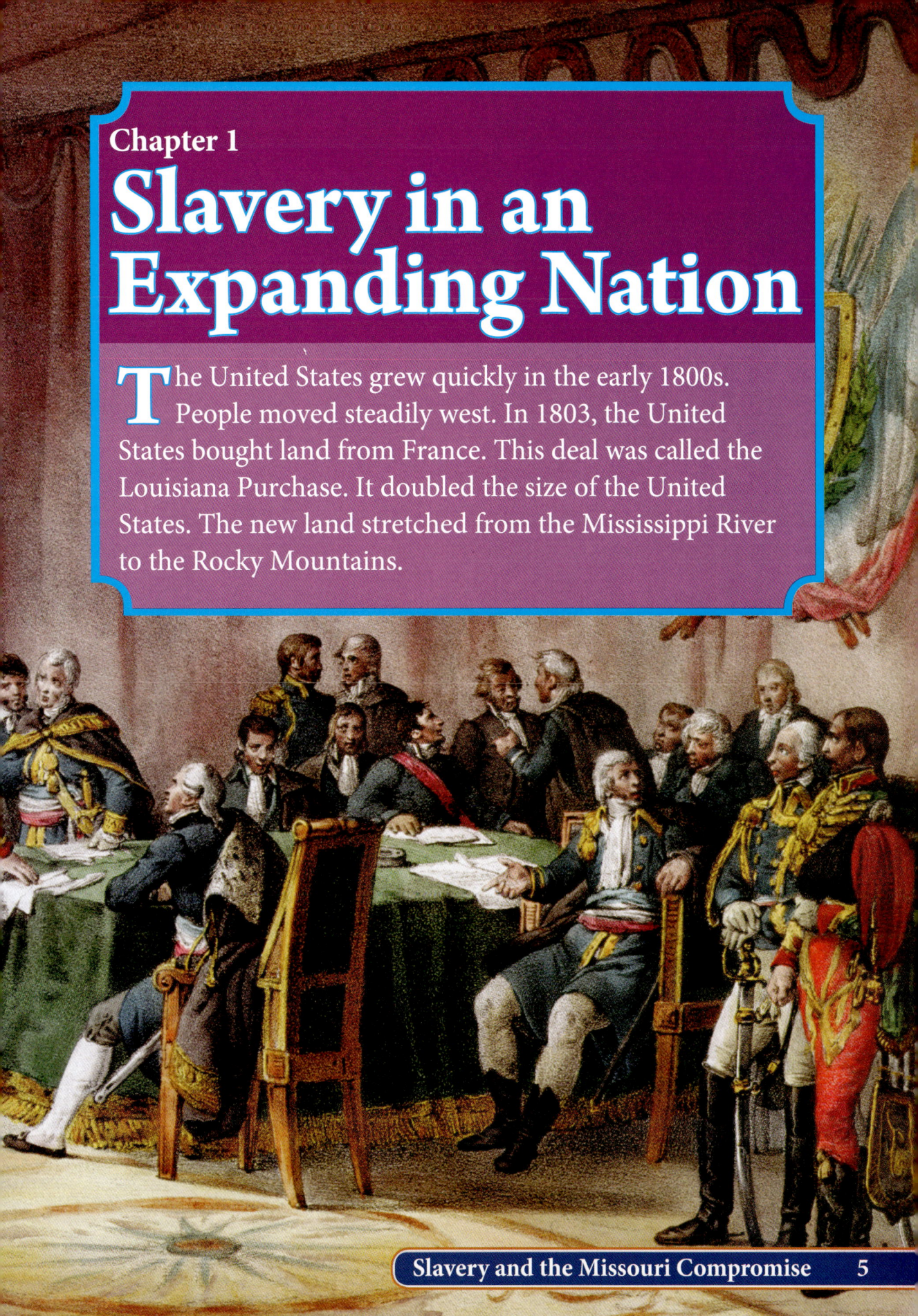

Chapter 1
Slavery in an Expanding Nation

The United States grew quickly in the early 1800s. People moved steadily west. In 1803, the United States bought land from France. This deal was called the Louisiana Purchase. It doubled the size of the United States. The new land stretched from the Mississippi River to the Rocky Mountains.

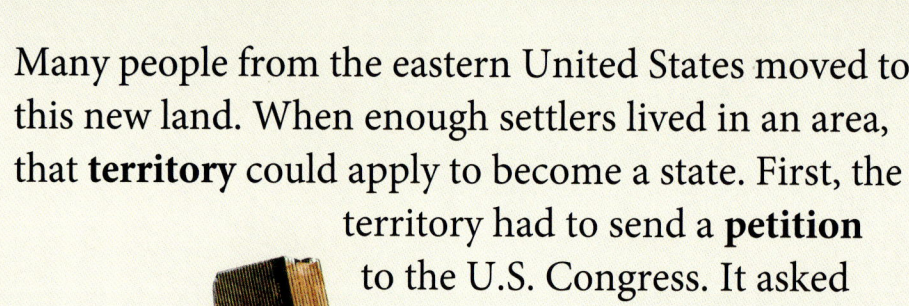

Many people from the eastern United States moved to this new land. When enough settlers lived in an area, that **territory** could apply to become a state. First, the territory had to send a **petition** to the U.S. Congress. It asked to become a state. Then members of Congress created a **bill**. They took a vote. If the bill passed, the territory would become a state.

As the country grew, people debated an important question. Should the new states allow slavery? This question divided the North and the South. Slavery was legal in southern states. They were known as slave states. Large farms in these states produced sugar and **cotton**.

The cotton gin, invented in 1793, and slave labor helped southern farms make money.

Demand for these products was increasing all over the world. And new inventions helped farms produce more. Many southern farms became large and powerful. But they depended on slavery. Without enslaved people, the farms would not make as much money. For this reason, southerners wanted the territories to become slave states.

In the North, states began passing laws to make slavery illegal. These were known as free states. Many northerners wanted the territories to become free states, too.

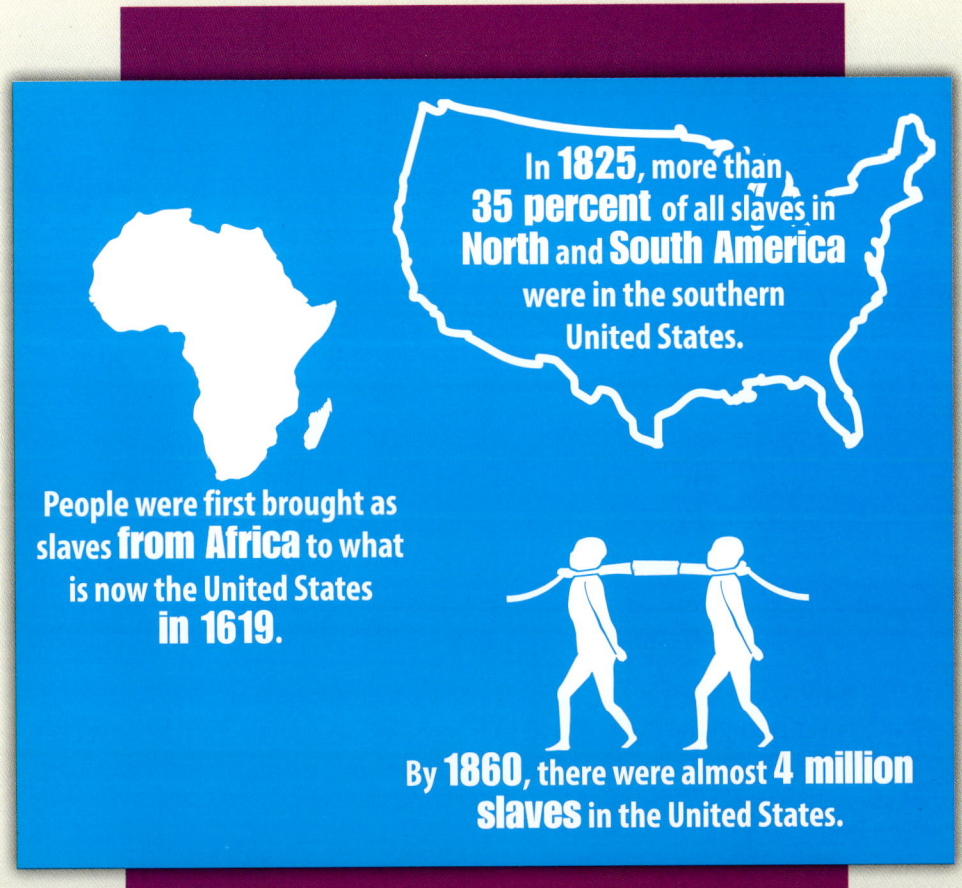

People were first brought as slaves **from Africa** to what is now the United States **in 1619**.

In **1825**, more than **35 percent** of all slaves in **North** and **South America** were in the southern United States.

By **1860**, there were almost **4 million slaves** in the United States.

Some northerners believed slavery was morally wrong. Others worried about slavery's **economic** effects. In free states, farmers paid their workers. But in slave states, farmers made slaves work without pay. Northerners thought this system gave southern farms an unfair advantage. Farms in the North could not compete.

Many white workers did not want slavery to spread. They wanted to work on farms and factories in the new lands. If slavery was allowed, farmers could use enslaved people instead. White workers worried that this would hurt their **wages**.

The Debate over Slavery

As new states became part of the United States, a fierce debate between slave and free states took place to determine their status.

1819
The Tallmadge **Amendment** is passed by the House of Representatives to make Missouri a free state. However, it stalls in the Senate.

1803
After the Louisiana Purchase, the size of the United States is roughly doubled.

1820
The Missouri **Compromise** is enacted by Congress to balance pro- and anti-slavery views.

Building Our Nation

Farmers in northern states often paid local people to harvest their crops. This added expenses not found in slave states.

1854

The Kansas–Nebraska Act, proposed by Stephen A. Douglas, allows "popular **sovereignty**" to determine whether or not a new state would have slaves.

1857

The Supreme Court declares the Missouri Compromise unconstitutional.

1861–1865

The U.S. Civil War takes place after the southern states leave the nation. The Thirteenth Amendment, ratified in 1865, ends slavery in the United States.

Slavery and the Missouri Compromise

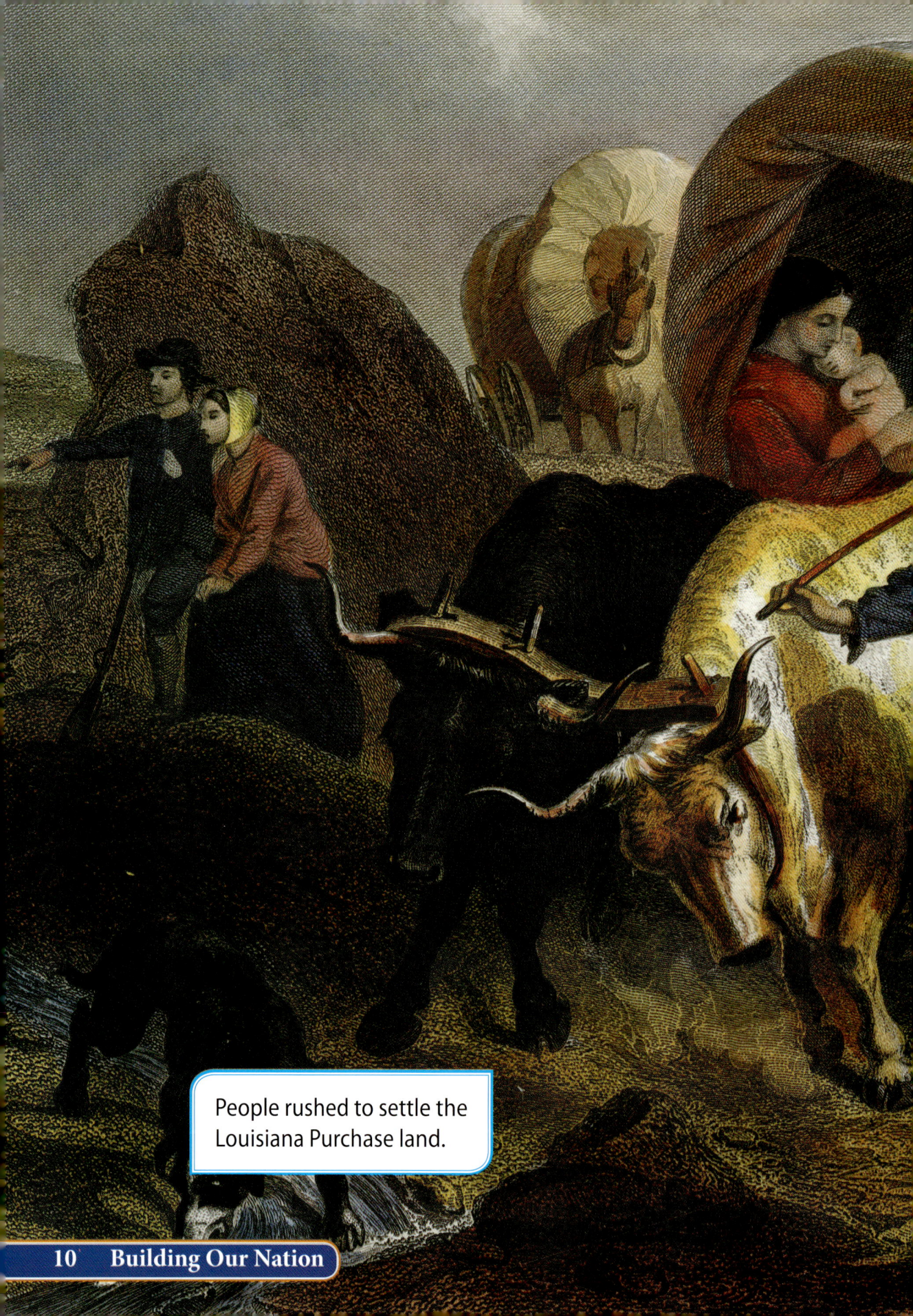

People rushed to settle the Louisiana Purchase land.

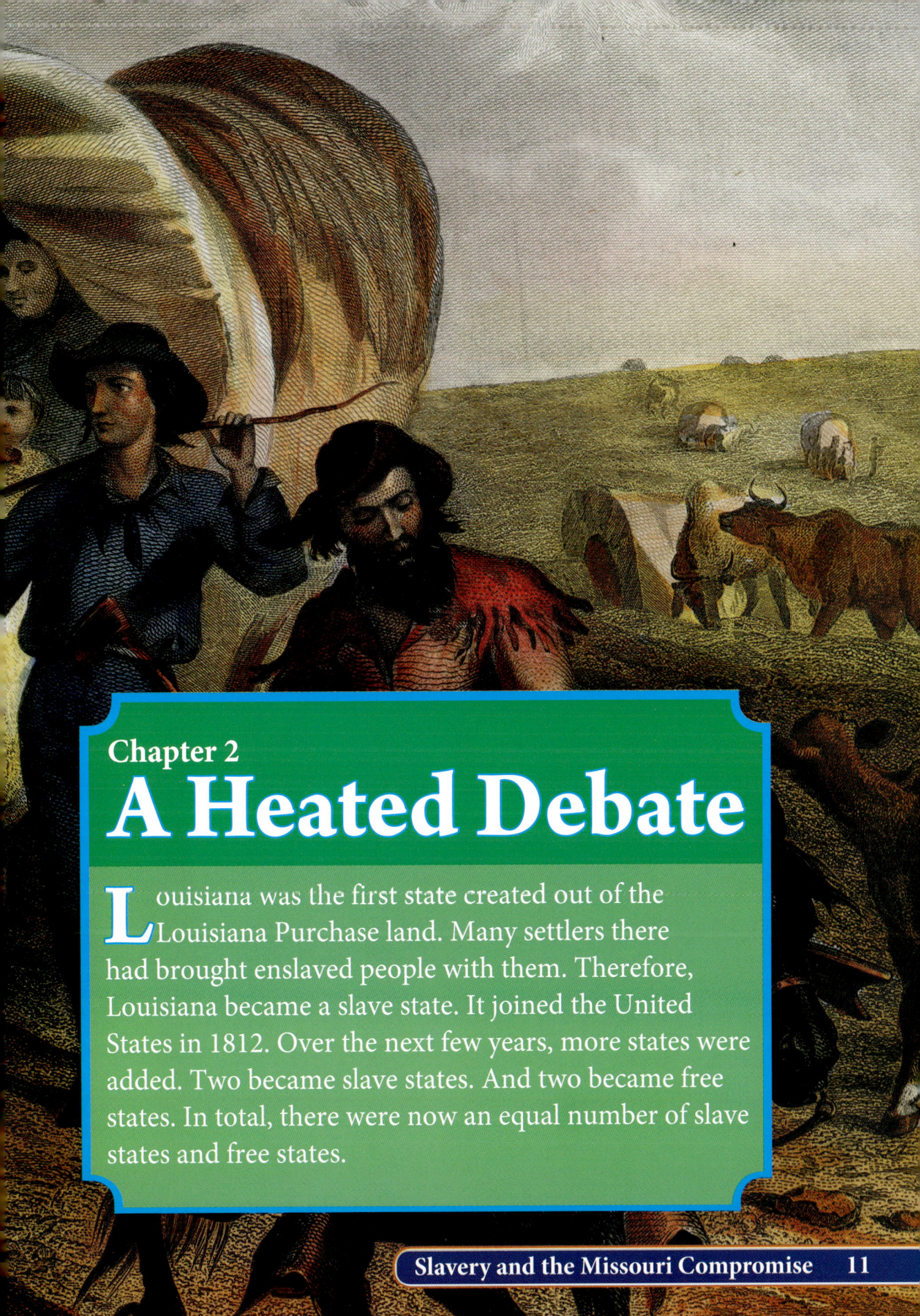

Chapter 2
A Heated Debate

Louisiana was the first state created out of the Louisiana Purchase land. Many settlers there had brought enslaved people with them. Therefore, Louisiana became a slave state. It joined the United States in 1812. Over the next few years, more states were added. Two became slave states. And two became free states. In total, there were now an equal number of slave states and free states.

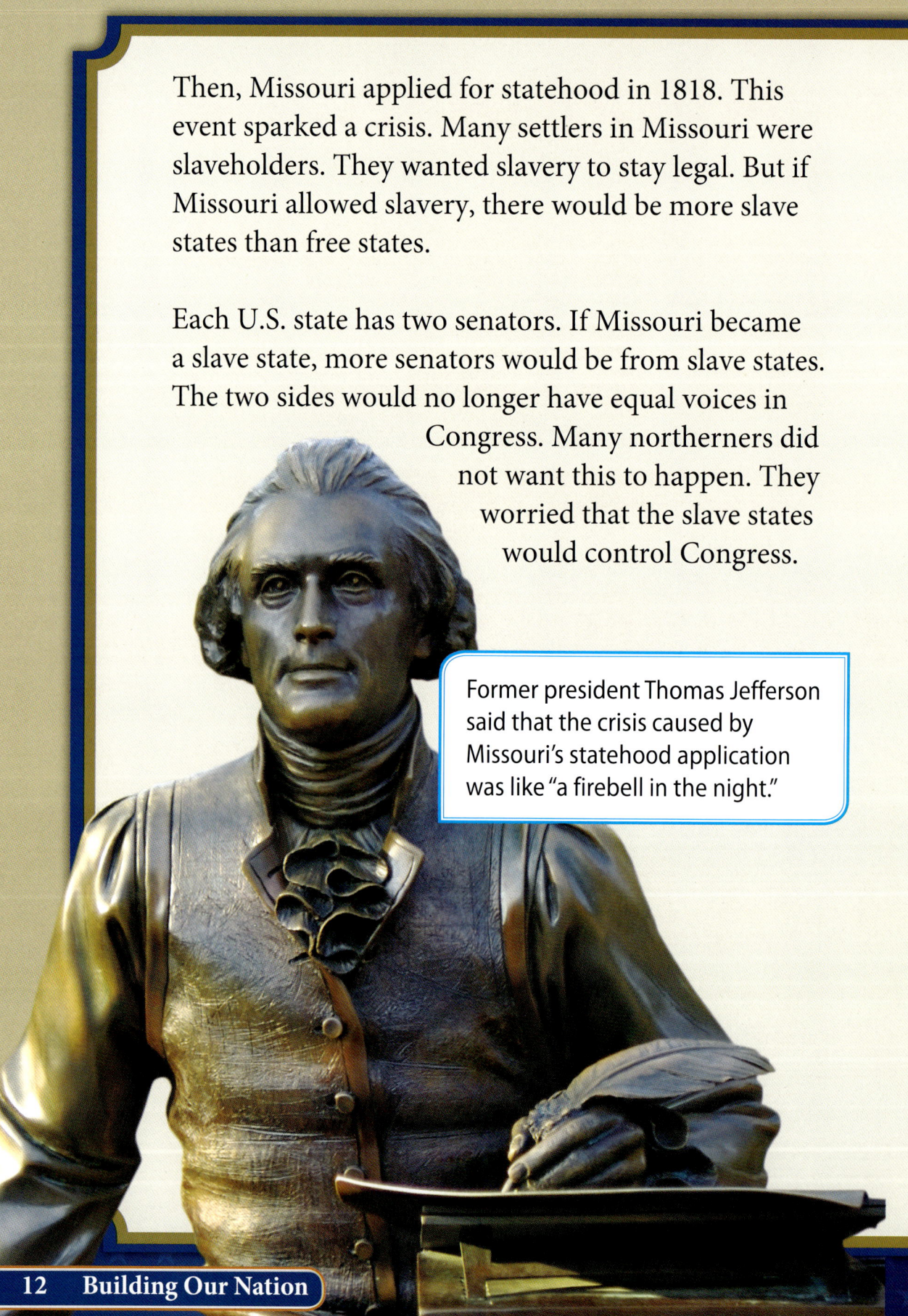

Then, Missouri applied for statehood in 1818. This event sparked a crisis. Many settlers in Missouri were slaveholders. They wanted slavery to stay legal. But if Missouri allowed slavery, there would be more slave states than free states.

Each U.S. state has two senators. If Missouri became a slave state, more senators would be from slave states. The two sides would no longer have equal voices in Congress. Many northerners did not want this to happen. They worried that the slave states would control Congress.

Former president Thomas Jefferson said that the crisis caused by Missouri's statehood application was like "a firebell in the night."

James Tallmadge served in the House of Representatives from 1817 to 1819.

James Tallmadge, a congressman from New York, tried to solve this problem. In 1819, he wrote an amendment to the Missouri statehood bill. The amendment would slowly put an end to slavery in the new state. Bringing any more enslaved people into Missouri would be illegal. In addition, the children of enslaved people would be freed when they turned 25 years old.

The amendment set off an angry debate. Southerners strongly opposed it. They argued that Congress could not make rules about slavery. Instead, they wanted each state to vote on the issue for itself.

Southerners also argued that Congress must respect slaveholders' rights. Many slaveholders had moved to Missouri from the South. They thought of enslaved people as their private property. In their view, making slavery illegal in Missouri would take away their property rights.

Northerners argued back. They did not want slavery to spread. The debate lasted for months. Both sides refused to back down. The debate threatened to split the nation. Finally, in February 1820, lawmakers suggested a compromise.

As a result of slave labor, many southern farmers became very wealthy.

Slave Population in the Southern States

During the period between 1790 and 1860, the population of enslaved people in the southern states increased by more than 3 million. Slaves made up about one third of the area's population during this time.

Year	Free Population	Slave Population
1790	1,272,977	654,121
1800	1,753,467	851,532
1810	2,215,398	1,103,700
1820	2,997,941	1,509,904
1830	3,789,674	1,983,860
1840	4,809,087	2,481,390
1850	6,420,298	3,200,364
1860	8,289,782	3,950,311

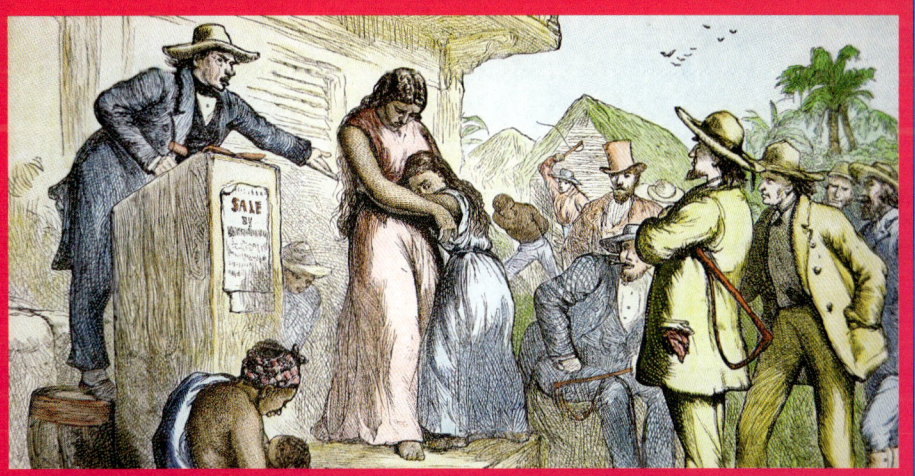

Slavery and the Missouri Compromise

The Missouri Compromise tried to get lawmakers from free states and slave states to stop fighting.

Chapter 3
Drawing a Line

The compromise had two parts. First, Maine would become a state at the same time as Missouri. At the time, Maine was part of Massachusetts. But it had applied to become a separate state. Maine would be a free state. Missouri would be a slave state. Adding two states would keep the balance of power.

Slavery and the Missouri Compromise

Second, Congress would draw an imaginary line through the Louisiana Purchase land. The line would follow the 36°30´ latitude line. This line runs along Missouri's southern border. Missouri would allow slavery. But slavery would not be allowed in any other land north of this line.

The Compromise was not popular at first. Southerners did not want to limit slavery. Northerners also opposed the compromise. Some did not want slavery to exist anywhere. Many thought the 36°30´ line was a bad choice. At the time, people thought most of the land north of this line was barren. If the land could not be used for farming, few people would want to settle there.

Henry Clay was known as "The Great Compromiser" for his skill at reaching agreements.

Henry Clay helped resolve the conflict. Clay was a congressman from Kentucky. He was a slaveholder. But he believed slavery was bad for the country. Clay wanted it to be slowly phased out. He also saw that the conflict was very serious. If left unsolved, it could split the nation.

Clay talked with many lawmakers. Some supported one part of the compromise but not the other. So, Clay divided the compromise into several bills. Congress voted separately on each bill. Each bill received enough votes to pass.

Monroe was elected president in 1816.

President James Monroe signed the Missouri Compromise into law in March 1820. But Missouri was not a state yet. Congress still had to approve Missouri's **constitution**. Part of its constitution said free black people could not enter the state. So, the anti-slavery members of Congress rejected it.

Once again, lawmakers argued. But Clay convinced them to accept another compromise. Missouri could keep its state constitution. But the state had to agree that its constitution could not be used to limit the rights of any U.S. citizen.

The Missouri Compromise

By introducing Maine as a free state and Missouri as a slave state at the same time, the Missouri Compromise helped clearly separate slave and free states while ensuring balance between the two types of states.

Slavery and the Missouri Compromise

The conflict over slavery only got worse as the United States continued to expand.

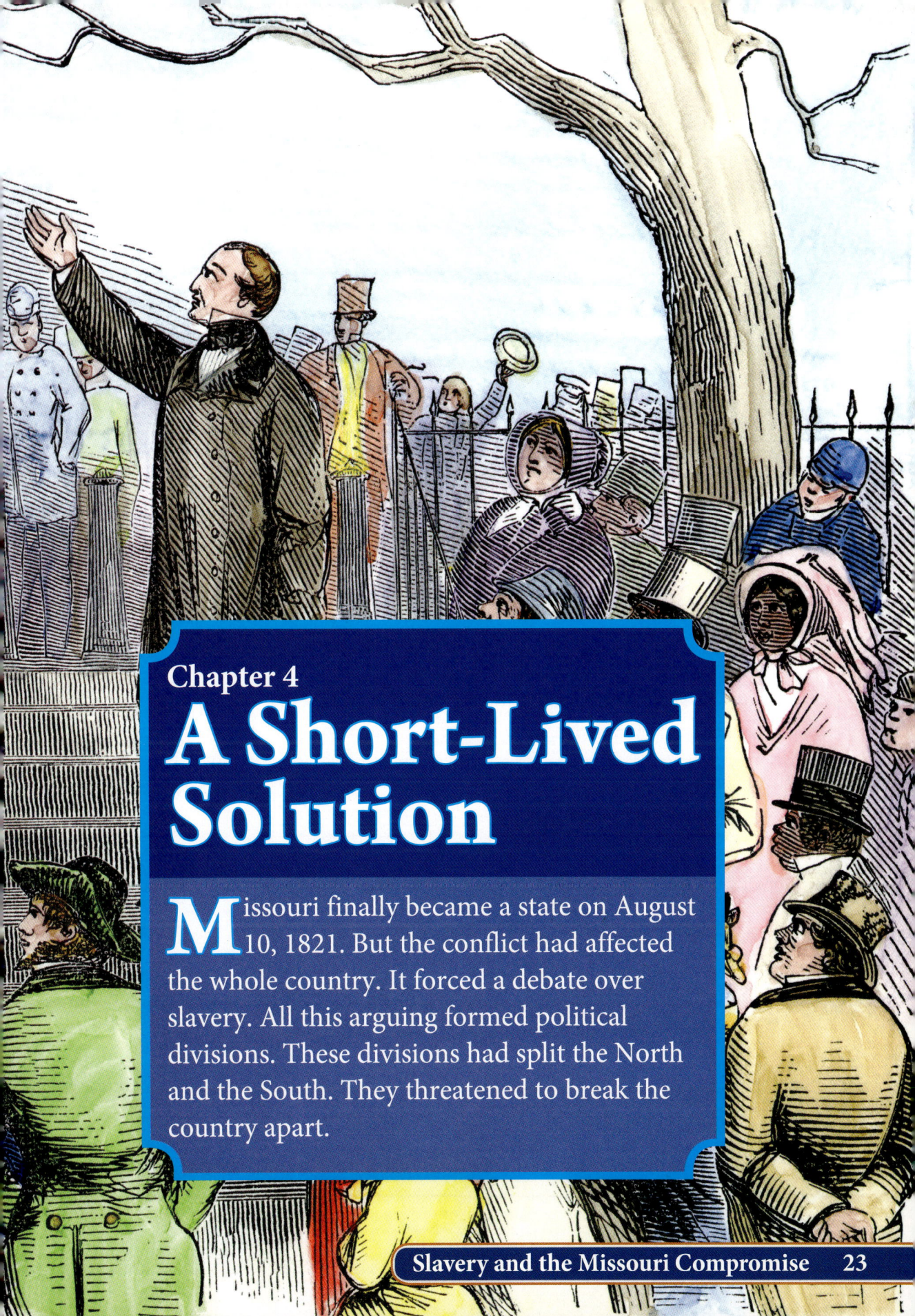

Chapter 4
A Short-Lived Solution

Missouri finally became a state on August 10, 1821. But the conflict had affected the whole country. It forced a debate over slavery. All this arguing formed political divisions. These divisions had split the North and the South. They threatened to break the country apart.

The Missouri Compromise of 1820 was only a temporary solution. The conflict over slavery continued. In 1854, Congress passed the Kansas–Nebraska Act. This law created the two new territories of Kansas and Nebraska.

Supporters of slavery crossed the Kansas–Missouri border to vote to make Kansas a slave state. Some voted illegally.

Kansas and Nebraska were part of the Louisiana Purchase land. Both were above the 36°30´ latitude line. According to the Missouri Compromise, they should have become free states. However, the Kansas–Nebraska Act allowed the territories to vote about slavery.

Kansas became a battleground. Many **abolitionists** settled there. They hoped their votes would make Kansas a free state. But pro-slavery people also moved into Kansas. The two sides clashed violently.

The Supreme Court dealt a final blow to the Missouri Compromise in 1857. The court took up the case of Dred Scott. Scott was enslaved. But he had lived in areas where the Missouri Compromise banned slavery. Therefore, Scott argued that he should be free.

Chief Justice Roger B. Taney wrote the majority opinion explaining the Supreme Court's reasoning in the Dred Scott case.

Most members of the Supreme Court were pro-slavery southerners. They ruled that the Missouri Compromise went against the U.S. Constitution. They said Congress did not have the power to ban slavery in the territories. They also said that as an enslaved person, Scott did not have any legal rights under the U.S. Constitution.

This decision deepened the country's divisions. Over the next four years, tensions grew. In 1861, the U.S. Civil War broke out. The Missouri Compromise had only delayed the crisis. Now, the divide had ripped apart the nation.

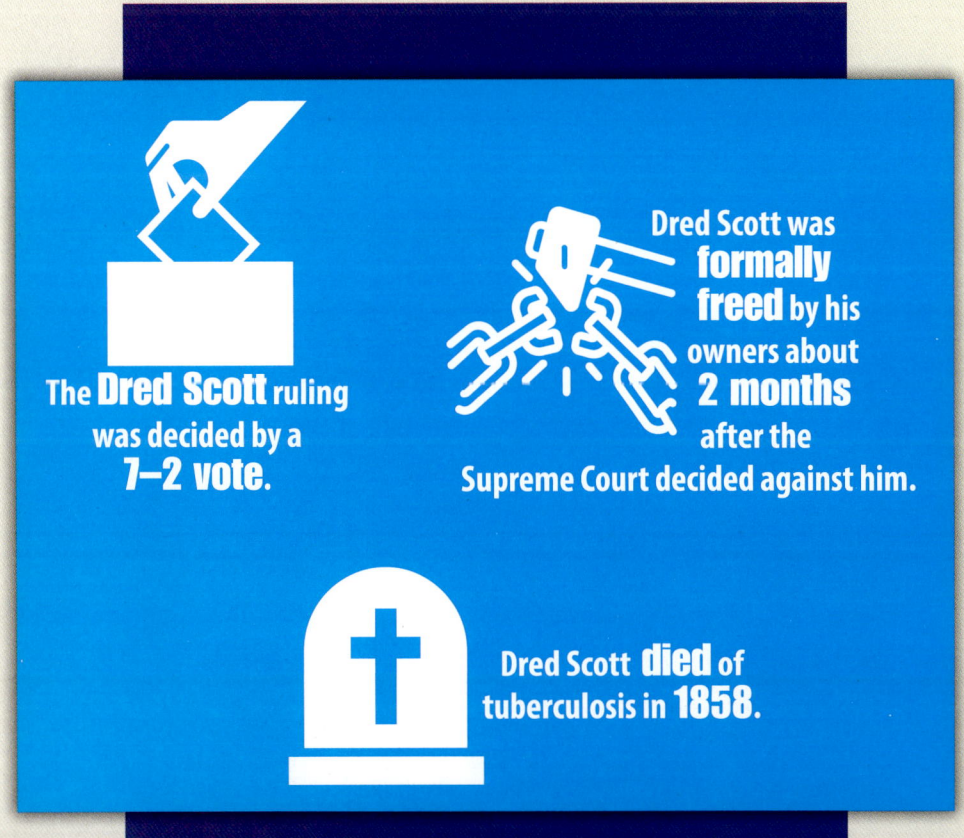

Voices From the Past

Frederick Douglass

The Kansas–Nebraska Act shocked abolitionists. This law had overturned, or ended, the Missouri Compromise. As a result, slavery could spread to areas where it had not been allowed before. Antislavery leaders strongly opposed this decision. One was Frederick Douglass.

Douglass grew up as a slave. When he was about 20 years old, he escaped. Douglass traveled and spoke out against slavery. He also worked and saved money to purchase his freedom. And in 1847, he started an anti-slavery newspaper.

Like many abolitionists, Douglass believed the Kansas–Nebraska Act was wrong. He said the decision "fell upon the nation like a bolt from a cloudless sky." He called people who agreed with it "the deadliest enemies of liberty."

However, Douglass remained hopeful. He thought the anti-slavery movement would continue to grow. "I have no fear for the ultimate triumph of free principles in this country," he said. "The progress of these principles has been constant, steady, strong, and certain."

Slavery and the Missouri Compromise

Quiz

1 What happened to the size of the United States after the Louisiana Purchase?

2 What overturned the Missouri Compromise?

3 When did Missouri apply for statehood?

4 When was the cotton gin invented?

5 Who was known as "The Great Compromiser"?

6 Who wrote the majority opinion in the Dred Scott case?

7 When did James Tallmadge serve in the House of Representatives?

8 How many slaves were in the United States by 1860?

Answer: 1. It was roughly doubled. **2.** The Kansas–Nebraska Act **3.** 1818 **4.** 1793 **5.** Henry Clay **6.** Chief Justice Roger B. Taney **7.** 1817 to 1819 **8.** Almost 4 million

Building Our Nation

Key Words

abolitionists: people who work to end slavery

amendment: a change added to a legal document

bill: a written plan to create or change a law

compromise: an agreement in which both sides give up something they want

constitution: a document laying out the basic beliefs and laws of a nation or state

cotton: a soft fabric made from plants

economic: having to do with the system of goods, services, money, and jobs in a certain place

petition: a formal request sent to an official person or group

sovereignty: power over a group of people

territory: an area of land that is not a state but is still part of the United States

wages: money that people receive for doing work

Index

abolitionists 26, 28

Clay, Henry 18, 19, 20, 30
constitution 21, 27

Douglass, Frederick 28, 29

free states 7, 8, 11, 12, 16, 17, 21, 25, 26

Kansas–Nebraska Act 9, 24, 25, 28, 30

Louisiana Purchase 4, 5, 8, 10, 11, 18, 21, 25, 30

Maine 17, 21
Mississippi River 5
Missouri 12, 13, 14, 15, 17, 18, 20, 23, 24, 26, 30
Missouri Compromise 8, 9, 16, 20, 21, 24, 25, 26, 27, 28, 30
Monroe, James 20

Rocky Mountains 5

Scott, Dred 26, 27, 30
slave states 6, 7, 8, 11, 12, 16, 17, 21, 24
Supreme Court 9, 26, 27

Tallmadge, James 13, 30

U.S. Civil War 9, 27
U.S. Congress 6, 8, 12, 13, 14, 18, 19, 20, 24, 27

Slavery and the Missouri Compromise

Log on to www.av2books.com

AV² by Weigl brings you media enhanced books that support active learning. Go to www.av2books.com, and enter the special code found on page 2 of this book. You will gain access to enriched and enhanced content that supplements and complements this book. Content includes video, audio, weblinks, quizzes, a slide show, and activities.

AV² Online Navigation

Audio
Listen to sections of the book read aloud.

Book Pages
AV² pages directly correspond to pages in the book.

Video
Watch informative video clips.

Key Words
Study vocabulary, and complete a matching word activity.

Embedded Weblinks
Gain additional information for research.

Try This!
Complete activities and hands-on experiments.

Quizzes
Test your knowledge.

Slide Show
View images and captions, and prepare a presentation.

AV² was built to bridge the gap between print and digital. We encourage you to tell us what you like and what you want to see in the future.

Sign up to be an AV² Ambassador at www.av2books.com/ambassador.

Due to the dynamic nature of the Internet, some of the URLs and activities provided as part of AV² by Weigl may have changed or ceased to exist. AV² by Weigl accepts no responsibility for any such changes. All media enhanced books are regularly monitored to update addresses and sites in a timely manner. Contact AV² by Weigl at 1-866-649-3445 or av2books@weigl.com with any questions, comments, or feedback.